Because
VOICE
is not a *single* sound

It's a
LIFETIME
echoing through.

AND THE WORDS *I've found*
have finally
led me back to... **ME.**

I AM NOT LESS— I am more now. A MOSAIC made of truth & fire. And I'll keep growing, GLOWING ON— with EVERY YEAR a little higher.

Every step forward IS MINE. EVERY SCAR. every win. I earned this joy, THIS MOMENT— Let the DANCING now begin.

I CRY when
something matters.
I fight when
SOMETHING'S
WRONG.

I celebrate
the fire I hold—
It's kept me
BOLD
THIS LONG.

This
SILENCE isn't lonely
It's not
retreat OR LACK.
It's the
ROOM I GIVE
my soul
TO BREATHE
when the
world
won't give it
BACK.

Some truths YOU ONLY find when you've run OUT of room To SHRINK

Turned toward the **JOY** that still breaks through—

In crumbs, in cracks, in time.

I may be **WILD. WORN.** AND A BIT undone...

But oh, this mess is mine.

But underneath,
A WILD COLOR
fought for
LIGHT

I'm made of
work
AND WONDER—
and
I carry both
WITH STYLE

It came with
years
AND SILENT
TEARS,
And days that
BROUGHT ME
TO MY
knees

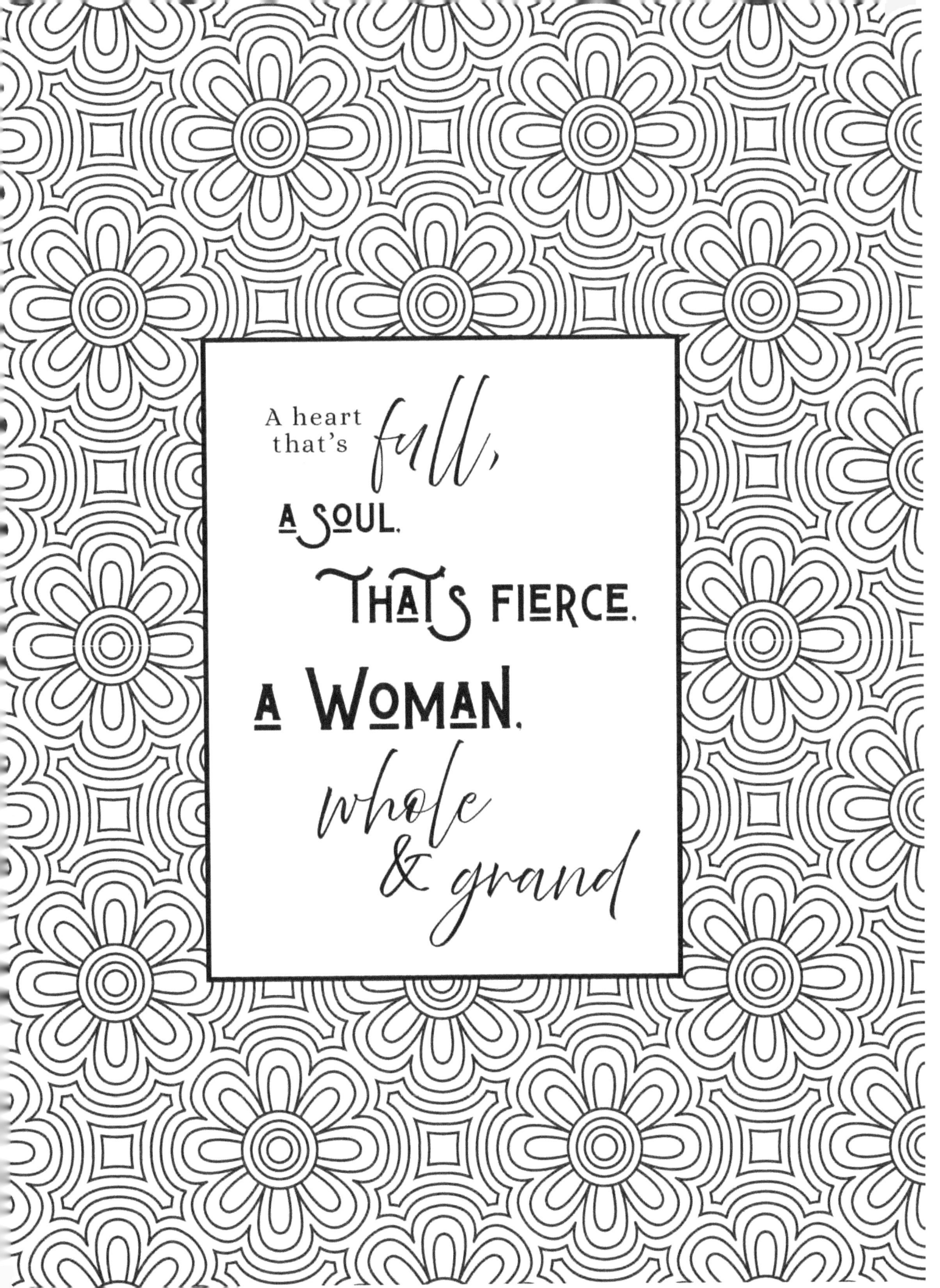

A heart that's *full,*
A SOUL.
THAT'S FIERCE.
A WOMAN.
whole
& grand

Some parts
of me WERE
ARMOR

Some were
masks
I had to wear.

Some got me
THROUGH
A WORLD
that
didn't always care.

I still make

WISHES...

not because *I need saving.*

BUT BECAUSE

I believe in

POSSIBILITY.

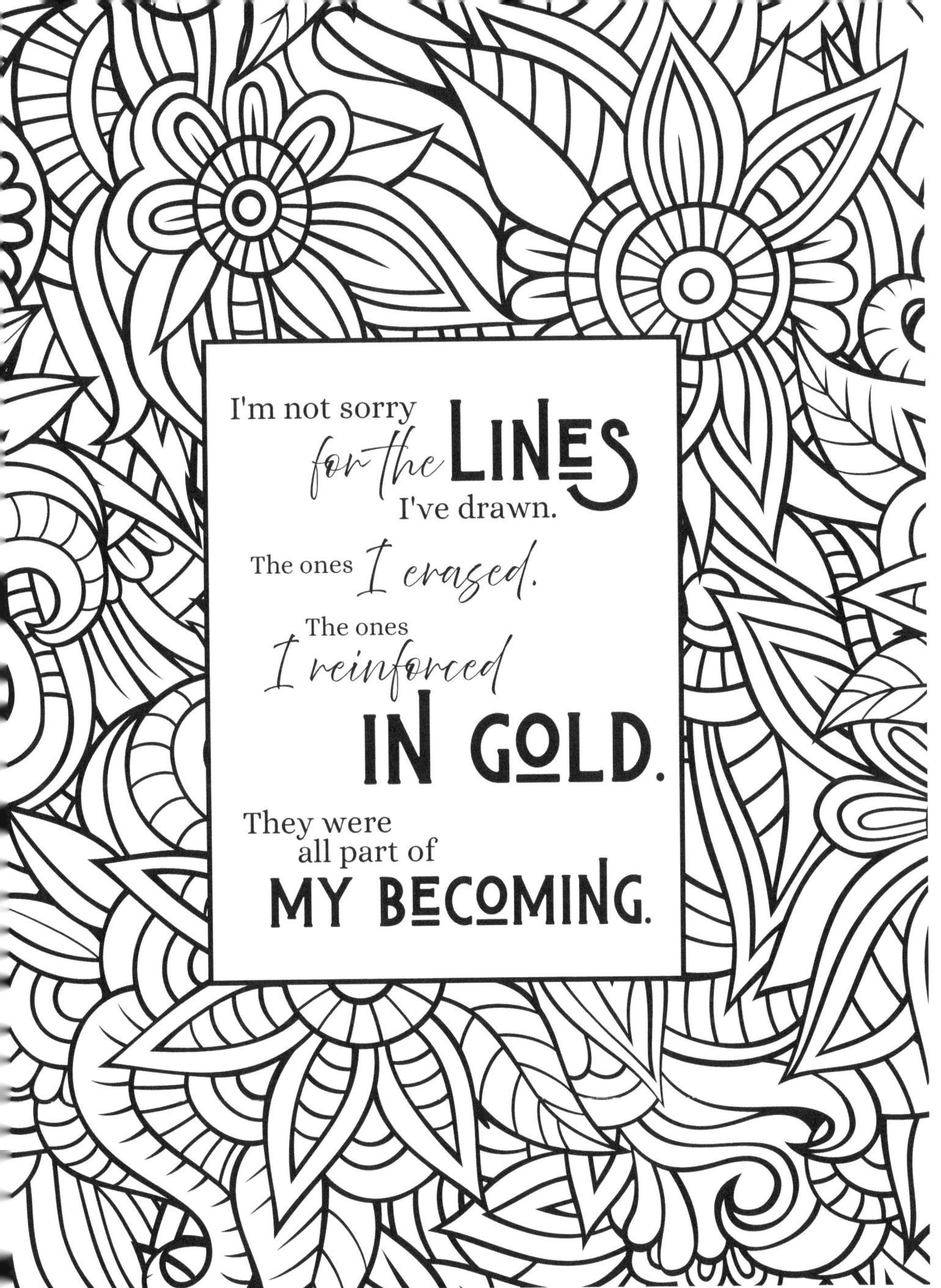

I'm not sorry for the LINES I've drawn.

The ones I erased.

The ones I reinforced IN GOLD.

They were all part of MY BECOMING.

But sometimes what **WE CARRY** is the *weight* of being **STRONG** too long

I carry
ALL THE COLORS
I've ever
worn
But I lead now
WITH
MY OWN

Becoming *sometimes* looks like LOSS before *it feels* COMPLETE

BOTH
QUIET STRENGTH
and
thunder
ARE POWER
I call my own.

I'm
exactly who
I'M MEANT
TO BE.